Picture Credits
t=top, tr=top right, tl=top left, bl= bottom left, br=bottom right, b=bottom, m=middle,
ml=middle left, mr=middle right

Front Cover Images: Anthony Findley; Cecil Sanders; Saguaro Pictures; Martin St-Amant;
User: Geographer; Sean Kennelly; Bev Sykes

Back Cover Images: Zac Wolf; Nimgsh M; Dimity Azovtsev; Shane Torgerson;
William Warby

Region Pages: P9: Mfwills (tr); P9: Rapidfire (b); P9: Diliff (mr); P16: Matt Kozlowski (bl);
P16: H. Michael Miley (bl); P17: J. Moliver (m); P17: Mali (b); P24: Ancheta Wis (ml); P24:
Sean Kennelly (bl,b); P24: Reid Priedhorsky (b); P25: Banpei (mr); P32:Saguaro Pictures
(m); P32: Averette (b); P32: Daniel Schwen (b) P36: Renjishino (tr); P36: Christian Abend
(mr); P36: Sean Kennelly (bl); P36: Diliff (br); P36: S Buckley (b); P37:C Heliker (tr);
P37: Joseph Plotz (ml); P37: Hajime Nakano (m); P37: Justforasecond (mr);
P37: Steve Jurvetson (b)

P10: Rob (bl); P10: PVSBond(bl); P11: Tony the Misfit (tr); P11: Xtremeyanksfan22 (bl); P11:
Gabor Eszes (b); P11: Wwkayaker22 (br); P12 UpstateNYer (l) ; P12: Postdfl (l); P12: William
Warby (m); P12: Jiuguang Wang (r); P12: Bob Jagendorf (br); P12: Connor Kurtz (dm); P13:
Cruadin (ml); P13: Telecasterman (m); P13: Thomsonsr (mr); P13: Makemake (br); P14:
Claude Covo-Farchi (ml); P14: Nadya Peek (m); P14: Gwernol (bl); P15: NHRHS2010 (ml);
P15: Amber Kincaid (mr); P15: M. Rehemtulla (mr); P15: Ben Franske (bl); P15: Jill Clardy
(bl); P15: Mfwills (m); P15: Raime (b); P18: Bill (ml); P18: Bbatsell (ml); P18: Nebular110
(m); P18: Nebular110 (bl); P18: JC Pollock (b); P19: Clemson3564 (ml); 19: Bubba73 (m);
19: Zac Wolf (b); P20: Derek Cashman (ml); P20: Stratosphere (m); P20: Daniel Schwen
(mr); P20: Beatrice M (mr); P20: Scott Basford (bl); P20: Cybjorg (bm); P20: Sean Russell
(br); P21: Rob Lavinsky (ml); P21: Doug Wertman (m); P21: Bobak (ml); P21: W. Marsh (bl);
P21: Bobak Ha'Eri (bm); P22: Ben Jacobson (bl); P22: Curtis Palmer (b); P23: Urban (mr);
P26: Coemgenus (ml); P26: Roger D. (ml); P26: Nick Nolte (m); P26: Andrew Hitchcock (mr);
P26: TheCadExpert (b); P26: Carey Akin (br); P27: BazookaJoe (ml); P27: Bardya (ml); P27:
Andrew Balet (m); P27: Nakor (mr); P27: Nimesh M (bl); P27: David Jones (b); P28: Laharl
(ml); P28: Tedder (m); P28: Richie Diesterheft (mr); P28: Reid Priedhorsky (b); P28: Rufus
Sarsaparilla (br); P29:Bill Whittaker (ml); P29: Bill Whittaker (mr); P29: Daniel Schwen (b);
P30: Bobak Ha'Eri (m); P30: Sean Kennelly (bl), (b); P31: Mike Tigas (ml); P31: FUBAR007
(bl); P31: Justin Hobson (b); P31: undergrounddarkride (b); P34: chensiyuan (m); P34:
Shane Torgerson (mr); P34: Daniel Mayer (b); P35: Mark Pellegrini (b); P38: Larry Johnson
(m); P38: Jsoo1 (mr); P38: Ahodges7 (b); P38: Massimo Catarinella (br); P39: S Buckley
(ml); P39: Martyn Jones (m); P39: Diliff (mr); P39: Christian Abend (br); P42: Skrewtape (ml);
P42: Sörn (m); P42: The Angels 2010 (m); P42: Mila Zinkova (m); P42: Dmitry Azovtsev (bl);
P42: Steve Jurvetson (b)

Series Editor:
Sean Kennelly

Written by
Sean Kennelly

Design by
Jonas Fearon Bell

Copyright © 2012 Flowerpot Press
a Division of Kamalu LLC, Franklin, TN, U.S.A.
and Mitso Media, Inc., Oakville, ON, Canada

Made in China/Fabriqué en Chine

CONTENTS

Looking for cool and interesting stuff? Watch for WOW facts on the pages of every World of Wonder book!

THESE UNITED STATES

From the very beginning, America has been a land filled with adventure, unique peoples and amazing sights.

The Early Settlements

English, French, and Spanish settlements dotted the shores of North America. The English claimed much of the Atlantic seacoast. The French claimed parts of the Deep South around what we know today as Louisiana. They also claimed land upriver through Missouri and further north in Canada. The Spanish claimed Florida and land to the southwest.

The First 13 and Beyond

America grew from the 13 English colonies. After winning its freedom from England, the young country grew and grew. It bought land from France called the Louisiana Purchase. It even bought a large chunk of snowy land from Russia which we called Alaska. It also fought wars with Spain over Texas and the western half of North America. It won the land from Spain along with Puerto Rico, the Philippines, and the island of Guam. After World War II, America gave the Philippines its independence, and now it is its own country. However, Guam and Puerto Rico are still part of the United States. They're called a U.S. territory.

YOU CALLED ME A WHAT?!

While most states are…well, states, there are some that are called a "commonwealth." We know them as the states of Kentucky, Virginia, Massachusetts and Pennsylvania. Why? All but Kentucky were part of the original 13 colonies. When they became independent, they wanted to change the name to show they were not run by a king. They were run by the "common" voice of the people. That meant everyone got to vote on laws and rules.

I VOTED

How are States Made?

States are areas of land located within the boundary of a country such as the United States of America. Most states start out as territories of the U.S. (except the original 13 colonies). When enough people want to become a state, they ask to be made a state. The government of the United States, or "Federal" Government, tells them to write a constitution – a set of rules or laws for their state. Once they do this, they send it back to the Federal Government. The government then votes to "admit" the state into the "Union." If it is admitted, it becomes an official state of the United States. Finally, the President proclaims it a state, and a new star is added to the U.S. flag!

What is Washington, D.C.?

The Founding Fathers of the United States did not want any state to have power over the capital city. So, Virginia and Maryland donated land to create a special district on the Potomac River, which was called the District of Columbia. The new capital city was named after George Washington, and it was built within the new District. Unlike a state, the District of Columbia is governed by the Federal Government. The only government it has is a mayor and a city council. The people also vote for a person to represent them in Congress, but its representative can't vote on federal laws. It may not seem fair, but that's life in the District!

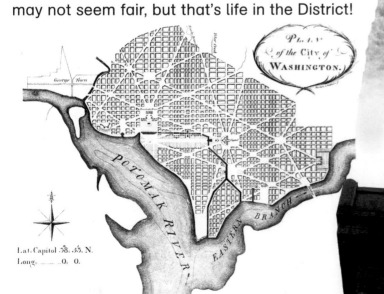

New England

The Northeast was the site of some of the earliest settlements. Most of the people who came in those early years were English Protestants. They were seeking a place where they would be free to practice their religion without interference from the government. They also believed strongly in the voice of the people and often held town meetings. At those meetings, everyone could participate in making laws to govern their communities. It's no wonder they began to resent being ruled by a king across the sea who wouldn't listen to their concerns.

The people of New England were a tough breed tasked with taming a tough land. They learned how to get things done when they had few resources. They valued education. They knew how important it was to work smarter. So it's no surprise they started a number of colleges and universities, beginning with Harvard in 1636. Yale, Dartmouth, and Brown are just a few of the other schools they started.

New England has also had a huge cultural influence on the country. Emily Dickenson, Edgar Allen Poe, Ralph Waldo Emerson, and Henry Wadsworth Longfellow are among the many writers and poets from the area. Of course, this could be partly due to the amount of time spent indoors in the winter. The bitter cold can be tough to weather unless you're busy skiing the slopes of the mountains of Vermont, New Hampshire, or Maine. Spring is filled with blossoms and green. Summers are a time to go to the beach to enjoy a good clam or lobster bake. And fall is a heavenly blanket of color as the leaves turn color.

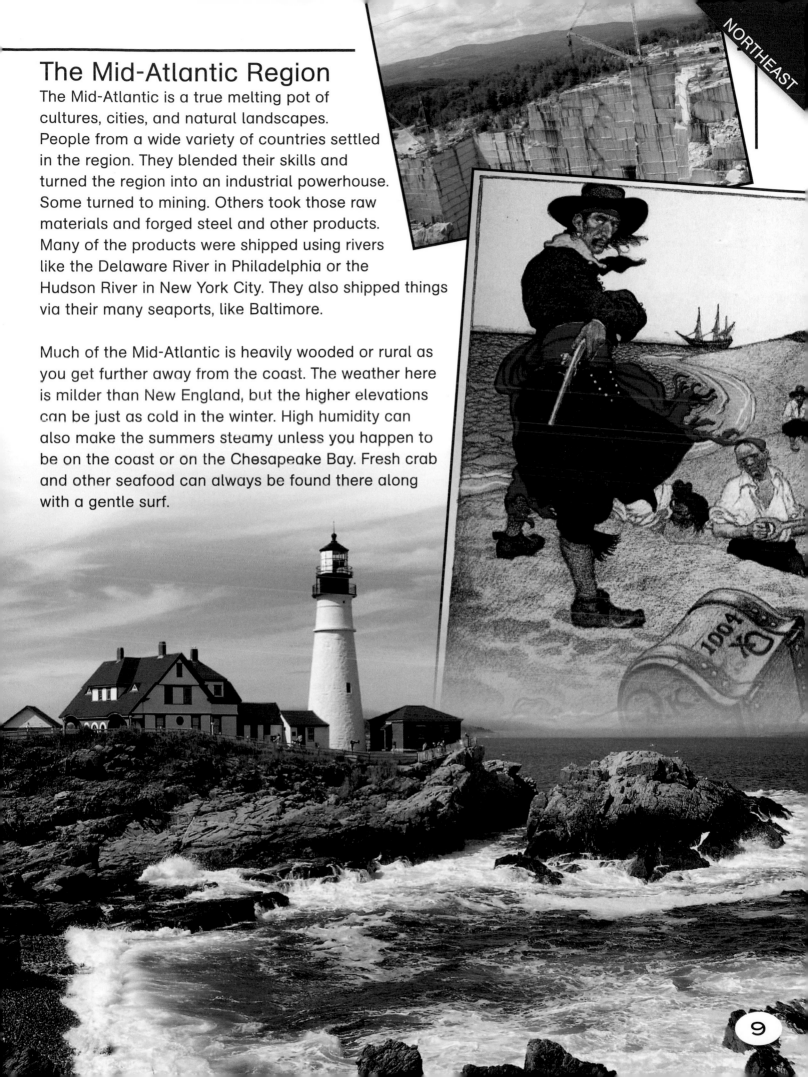

The Mid-Atlantic Region

The Mid-Atlantic is a true melting pot of cultures, cities, and natural landscapes. People from a wide variety of countries settled in the region. They blended their skills and turned the region into an industrial powerhouse. Some turned to mining. Others took those raw materials and forged steel and other products. Many of the products were shipped using rivers like the Delaware River in Philadelphia or the Hudson River in New York City. They also shipped things via their many seaports, like Baltimore.

Much of the Mid-Atlantic is heavily wooded or rural as you get further away from the coast. The weather here is milder than New England, but the higher elevations can be just as cold in the winter. High humidity can also make the summers steamy unless you happen to be on the coast or on the Chesapeake Bay. Fresh crab and other seafood can always be found there along with a gentle surf.

MARYLAND (1788)

Old Line State / Free State

Capital: Annapolis
Abbreviation: MD
Population (2010): 5,773,552
Total Area: 10,441 sq. mi. (27,042 sq. km)
State Motto: "Fatti Maschii, Parole Femine (Manly Deeds, Womanly Words)"
State Bird: Baltimore Oriole
State Flower: Black-Eyed Susan
Sights to See: Eastern Shores/Assateague Island Wild Ponies, Baltimore Harbor/Ft. McHenry (site of the 1814 battle that inspired "The Star-Spangled Banner"; Annapolis – Sailing Capital of America

Maryland was called the "Old Line State" by George Washington for the Maryland Line: the soldiers from the state who fought in the Revolutionary War. Being a coastal state, it is well-known for its seafood, sailing and the U.S. Naval Academy. The famous novel, *Misty of Chincoteague*, by Marguerite Henry was written about the wild ponies that reside on Assateague and Chincoteague Island. Each year, some of the ponies are rounded up and swim to the mainland to be auctioned to the public.

DELAWARE (1787)

First State / Diamond State

Delaware was the first state to ratify the U.S. Constitution and thus earned the name, the "First State." One of the state's early settlers, the Swedish, built the first log cabins in America in Delaware. The capital of Dover also boasts a historic horse racing track and a NASCAR raceway nicknamed the "Monster Mile." The raceway even has a glass section (the Monster Bridge) where you can sit over the track and watch the race! Of course, if you want to see one of the most amazing gardens in the country, Longwood Gardens is the place. The gardens started as a farm way back in 1700. In the 1800s, an arboretum (a garden for trees) was created by the Pierce brothers. Then in 1906, Pierre du Pont took the money he made from his family business (the famous DuPont Company) and created a garden like no other with dazzling fountains. You have to see it!

Capital: Dover
Abbreviation: DE
Population (2010): 897,934
Total Area: 2,023 sq. mi. (5,240 sq. km)
State Motto: "Liberty and Independence"
State Bird: Blue Hen Chicken
State Flower: Peach Blossom
Sights to See: Dover Downs/Dover International Speedway, Longwood Gardens, Delaware Beaches

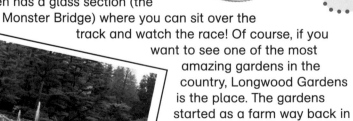

PENNSYLVANIA (1787)

Keystone State

The Keystone State got its nickname from its central role in creating the new country of America. It has been the place where the Declaration of Independence was signed as well as the U.S. Constitution. In fact, Philadelphia was the first U.S. capital. And who can resist the taste of a real Philly Cheese Steak sandwich? With one of the largest populations in the U.S., Pennsylvania is home to a variety of people including the rural Amish and Mennonite communities (much of the state is rural). Pennsylvania also knows how to work hard and play hard. That explains how a city like Pittsburgh is home to both industrial steel mills, winning football teams and the roller coasters of historic Kennywood Amusement Park. But if you want to visit one of the sweetest places on earth, you have to see Hershey, PA. It's where one of the world's largest chocolate factories has been making sweets for over a century. Just be sure to visit Punxsutawney on February 2nd for Ground Hog Day!

WEST VIRGINIA (1863)

Mountain State

Originally part of Virginia, West Virginia disagreed with its brothers to the South. It was admitted to the Union during the Civil War. Located in the midst of the Appalachian Mountains, it is called the "Mountain State" because it has the highest average elevation of any state east of the Mississippi River. The land is filled with gas and coal pockets making West Virginia one of the best coal-mining sites in the world. But it's the natural beauty of West Virginia that attracts most visitors. Whitewater rafting adventure can be found in the rivers, and the high mountains offer snow skiing in the winter. Truly, West Virginia is an untamed beauty!

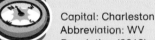

New York (1788)

Empire State

One of the largest colonies next to Virginia, New York has always been a big part of America. New York City, or the "Big Apple" (its nickname), is the biggest city in the United States. It is home to a wide range of cultures and nationalities that call America home. New York is also known for its manufacturing – everything from scientific technology to clothing. Western New York is much more rural with the Hudson River Valley cutting through the Adirondack Mountains on its 300-mile journey to the Atlantic Ocean. Of course, one of New York's most stunning sights, Niagara Falls, can be found near the Canadian border. It is the oldest state park in America where 3,160 tons of water flows over the falls every second!

Capital. Albany
Abbreviation: NY
Population (2010): 19,378,102
Total Area: 53,095 sq. mi. (137,515 sq. km)
State Motto: "Excelsior (Ever Upward)"
State Bird: Eastern Bluebird
State Flower: Rose
Sights to See: New York City – Statue of Liberty, Times Square, World Trade Center Memorial, Brooklyn Bridge, Empire State Building; Niagara Falls; Catskill Mountains; Adirondack Mountains

New Jersey (1787)

Garden State

New Jersey was originally named after England's Isle of Jersey, but it's no island. It is surrounded by the Hudson River, the Delaware River, and the Atlantic Ocean. However, it also shares a 50-mile land border with New York. New Jersey also has a number of fun places to visit. There are great beaches, from historic Cape May to the famous Atlantic City boardwalk. Or you can just float down the Delaware River. New Jersey is also the site of the very first baseball game in 1846, as well as the first college football game in 1869. The first dinosaur skeleton in North America was also discovered in New Jersey. So you could call New Jersey a land of firsts!

Capital: Trenton
Abbreviation: NJ
Population (2010): 8,791,894
Total Area: 7,812 sq. mi. (20,233 sq. km)
State Motto: "Liberty and Prosperity"
State Bird: Eastern Goldfinch
State Flower: Blue Violet
Sights to See: Cape May; Atlantic City (Steel Pier); Ocean City; Pilesgrove – Cowtown Rodeo; Burlington – Historical District; Jersey City – Liberty State Park; Camden – USS New Jersey Battleship & Museum

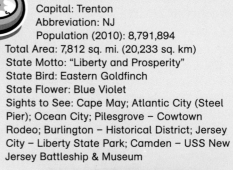

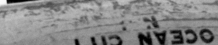

RHODE ISLAND (1790)
Little Rhodie / Ocean State

- Capital: Providence
- Abbreviation: RI
- Population (2010): 1,052,567
- Total Area: 1,221 sq. mi. (3,162 sq. km)
- State Motto: "Hope"
- State Bird: Rhode Island Red chicken
- State Flower: Violet
- Sights to See: Narragansett – Narragansett Town Beach; Newport – Castle Hill Lighthouse; Block Island; Providence – Roger Williams National Memorial; North Kingstown – Casey Farm; Jamestown – Beavertail State Park

Rhode Island was actually discovered by Italian explorer Giovanni da Verrazano in 1524. He was trying to get to France and reached Rhode Island's Narragansett Bay instead. Beautiful Narragansett Bay is home to many islands where Americans love to vacation year after year. Of course, fishing also has a long tradition in Rhode Island. Though it's true that Rhode Island is the smallest state, its capital city, Providence, is the second biggest city in New England behind Boston, MA. The state is also home to many factories that make toys, machines, silverware, and even costume jewelry. Believe it or not, the state bird is actually a breed of chicken (Rhode Island Red). Rhode Islanders are no chickens. It's a very brave state. Back in 1776, it was the first to declare its independence from England!

CONNECTICUT (1788)
Constitution State / Nutmeg State

Wherever you turn, Connecticut is filled with great places and great stories! The Old Newgate Prison in Granby was a copper mine that was turned into a prison back in the 1700s. It's said that the spooky ghosts of old prisoners and doomed miners wander its tunnels. Then there is the Mystic Seaport with its recreation of a historic New England seaport and the Mark Twain House (the author's favorite place to live) in Hartford. You can even go inside the U.S.S. *Nautilus* at the Navy Submarine Museum in Groton. Of course, no visit to Connecticut would be complete without a visit to Yale University (founded in 1701) and its Great Hall of Dinosaurs at the Peabody Natural History Museum.

- Capital: Hartford
- Abbreviation: CT
- Population (2010): 3,574,097
- Total Area: 5,004 sq. mi. (12,960 sq. km)
- State Motto: "Qui Transtulit Sustinet (He Who Transplanted, Sustains)"
- State Bird: American Robin
- State Flower: Mountain Laurel
- Sights to See: Pizza, Mystic Seaport Museum; Hartford – Harriet Beecher Stowe House, Mark Twain House; Yale University – Peabody Natural History Museum; New London – U.S. Coast Guard Academy; East Granby – The Old Newgate Prison; Groton – U.S. Navy Submarine Museum

MAINE (1820)

Pine Tree State

Did you know that Maine was once part of Massachusetts? It was, and it became a state in 1820 as part of the "Missouri Compromise." It made Maine a "free" state to balance out the new "slave" state of Missouri. It was called the Pine Tree State because 90% of Maine is covered in forests. So if you like the great outdoors, then you might consider Maine an outdoor paradise! You could visit Acadia National Park (the nation's smallest national park). See the 40-acre "Desert" of Maine, an ancient glacial sand deposit. Or take a ride on the Maine Narrow Gauge Railroad along Portland's waterfront where you can see the Portland Head Light (built in 1791) – the oldest U.S. lighthouse in use. And be sure to try the lobster. More lobster is caught off Maine's coast than any other state!

Capitul: Augusta
Abbreviation: ME
Population (2010): 1,328,361
Total Area: 33,123 sq. mi. (85,788 sq. km)
State Motto: "Dirigo (I Lead)"
State Bird: Black-Capped Chickadee
State Flower: White Pine Cone and Tassel
Sights to See: Palace Playland; Acadia National Park; Portland – Maine Narrow Gauge Railroad, Portland Head Light; Kennebunkport – Seashore Trolley Museum; Augusta – Old Fort Western

NEW HAMPSHIRE (1788)

Granite State

General John Stark of New Hampshire once said, "Live free or die," on the anniversary of the Revolutionary War's Battle of Bennington. So his home state adopted the phrase as its motto. History comes alive in New Hampshire at places like The Brick Store – America's oldest general store. Or drive through the many covered bridges along the way. If you have a sweet tooth, you may want to check out Sweet Maples Sugarhouse to see how maple tree sap becomes syrup. You can also go moose watching on State Route 3, or Moose Alley as it's called. But for the best view, ride the Cog Railway to the top of Mount Washington – the highest point in the Northeast and the windiest on earth! It once had a recorded wind speed of 231 mph (372 kmh)!

Capital: Concord
Abbreviation: NH
Population (2010): 1,316,470
Total Area: 9,280 sq. mi. (24,035 sq. km)
State Motto: "Live Free or Die"
State Bird: Purple Finch
State Flower: Purple Lilac
Sights to See: Pittsburg – Moose Alley (State Route 3); Covered Bridges; Mount Washington Cog Railway; Bath – The Brick Store; Dartmouth College; Salem – Stonehenge USA; Newbury – Sweet Maples Sugarhouse; Charlestown – Fort at No 4, Mount Monadnock

VERMONT (1791)
Green Mountain State

Capital: Montpelier
Abbreviation: VT
Population (2010): 625,741
- Total Area: 9,617 sq. mi. (24,908 sq. km)
- State Motto: "Freedom and Unity"
- State Bird: Hermit Thrush
- State Flower: Red Clover
- Sights to See: Killington; Waterbury – Ben & Jerry's Factory; Graniteville – world's largest active rock quarry; Pittsford – New England Maple Museum

Ethan Allen and the Green Mountain Boys (the volunteer soldiers of Vermont) fought bravely in the Revolutionary War. They got their name from the green mountains found in the state. However, Vermont was not one of the original colonies and became the 14th state in 1791. Today, Vermont is known for much more. It is the biggest producer of maple syrup in the country. It also has over 100 covered bridges throughout the state. You can find the world's biggest, active, granite quarry in…Graniteville. In the summer, you'll want to drop by the Ben & Jerry's factory in Waterbury. And if it's winter, you might want to strap on some skis and head for Killington. It's one of the top snow skiing destinations in America!

MASSACHUSETTS (1788)
Bay State / Old Colony State

From the day the Pilgrims arrived at Plymouth Rock, Massachusetts has been an important part of American history. The Boston Massacre and the Boston Tea Party happened here. It's the land of Paul Revere's midnight ride where he warned, "The British are coming!" Well, if you're coming by sea, you may want to visit the island of Martha's Vineyard. Many of the rich and famous (including many U.S. presidents) vacation there every year. If you're coming by land, you may want to stop by Provincetown where the wreck of the pirate treasure ship, Whydah, is on display with all its loot!

Capital: Boston
Abbreviation: MA
Population (2010): 6,547,629
- Total Area: 8,262 sq. mi. (21,398 sq. km)
- State Motto: "Ense Petit Placidam Sub Libertate Quietem (By the Sword We Seek Peace, But Peace Only Under Liberty)"
- State Bird: Black-Capped Chickadee
- State Flower: Mayflower (Trailing Arbutus)
- Sights to See: Plymouth Rock; Boston – Freedom Trail (Old North Church, U.S.S. *Constitution*); Cambridge – Harvard University; Cape Cod/Martha's Vineyard; Provincetown – Expedition Whydah Pirate Museum

The South

The Mason-Dixon Line is a line that was mapped out by Charles Mason and Jeremiah Dixon in 1767. The line created the borders of Pennsylvania, Maryland, Delaware, and Virginia. The states to the south took part of the name and called it "Dixie." Dixie thrived on cotton, sugar, tobacco, and the plantations that grew them until the American Civil War. At the root of the war was the issue of slavery. And the South depended on slaves to do most of the work on the plantations.

At the end of the Civil War, the slaved were freed. Plantations began to disappear. Smaller farms began to take their places. It wasn't until the 1900s that the South finally rose from the ashes of the Civil War to become prosperous again. The invention of air conditioning helped, too. People began to leave the cold winters of the north behind and head south. Today, the region is, once again, a powerhouse of agriculture and industry. And the natural beauty that has always graced the South can still be found in Dixie!

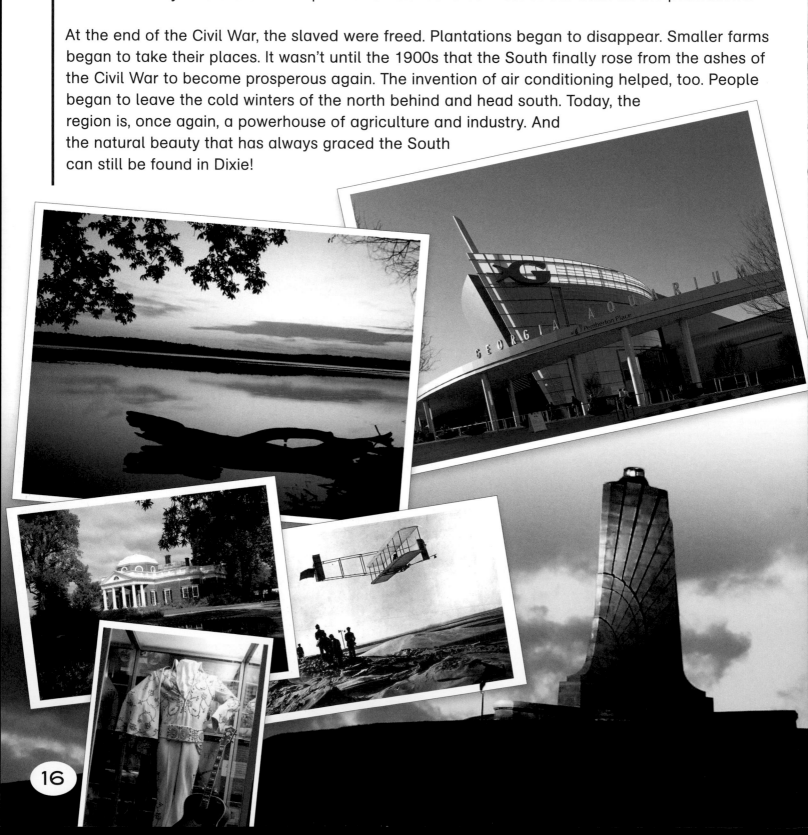

Tropical America

Not many people are aware that America extends beyond the tip of Florida. A highway links Florida to a chain of tropical islands called the Florida Keys. A "key" is another name for a small island. Key West is the southern-most island. To get there, you only need a car since the entire chain is connected by U.S. Route 1 over a series of bridges they call the "Overseas Highway." The longest bridge is called the Seven Mile Bridge because…it's seven miles long!

Puerto Rico and the U.S. Virgin Islands are American territories, and the people living there are U.S. citizens. Remember, many states start as territories then become states. Puerto Rico has voted many times on becoming a state. Each time, the majority of the people decided they wanted to stay a commonwealth.

The U.S. Virgin Islands were originally called the Danish West Indies before they were purchased by the United States. But the new name never changed the Islands much. It continues to thrive on tourists seeking a sunny, Caribbean vacation.

VIRGINIA (1788)
Mother of Presidents / Old Dominion

Virginia was once called the Dominion and Colony of Virginia since its territory made up what is now the states of West Virginia, Ohio, Kentucky, Indiana, Illinois, Wisconsin, and part of Minnesota. Many famous battles have been fought here, and both the Revolutionary War and the Civil War were ended in this state. Virginia has also been the home of many U.S. presidents. George Washington, Thomas Jefferson, James Madison, James Monroe, William Henry Harrison, John Tyler, Zachary Taylor, and Woodrow Wilson all lived here. It's not surprising since it's a land of beauty and variety. From Virginia Beach ("world's longest pleasure beach") to Skyline Drive in the Blue Ridge Mountains, there are stunning sights at every turn.

NORTH CAROLINA (1789)
Tar Heel State / Old North State

Many people called North Carolina the Tar Heel State for the way its Civil War soldiers stuck to their position like they had tar on their heels. Yet its license plate proudly proclaims "First In Flight," since the Wright Brothers made their famous flights among the sand dunes of the Outer Banks. Edward Teach, a.k.a. Blackbeard, also used the Outer Banks as his base of operations. He would often hide his ship near Ocracoke Island and attack passing boats. Today, visitors come to enjoy the beaches, the lighthouses (like Cape Hatteras), or the beauty of the mountain regions. In fact, a modern recreation of a French chateau can be found in Asheville. There George Vanderbilt built his famous Biltmore Mansion – the largest home in the U.S. with 250 rooms!

SOUTH CAROLINA (1788)

Palmetto State

South Carolina has always had plenty of visitors. It's said that Blackbeard once blocked the port of Charlestown until it paid the ransom he demanded. During the Revolutionary War, Francis Marion spent his time in the swamps. From there he struck British troops who named him the "Swamp Fox." Union soldiers even made Hilton Head Island their base of operations during the Civil War. They were there to fight the Rebels who first struck at Fort Sumter. Modern visitors to South Carolina now come to the sunny shoreline of Myrtle Beach. Some come to challenge the rapids of the Chattooga River near the Georgia border. Whatever the reason, it seems South Carolina has something for everyone!

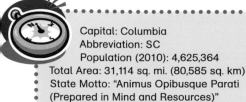

Capital: Columbia
Abbreviation: SC
Population (2010): 4,625,364
Total Area: 31,114 sq. mi. (80,585 sq. km)
State Motto: "Animus Opibusque Parati (Prepared in Mind and Resources)"
State Bird: Carolina Wren
State Flower: Yellow Jessamine
Sights to See: Charlestown – Arthur Ravenel, Jr. Bridge, Historic District; Fort Sumter; Myrtle Beach; Hilton Head Island; Chattooga River – whitewater rafting; The Citadel; Table Rock State Park

GEORGIA (1788)

Empire State of the South / Peach State

Georgia is home to a wide range of historical and natural marvels. The old coastal port of Savannah has been called one of the most haunted cities in America. It even boasts an old pirate tavern from the 1700s! Then there's Atlanta with its "Underground" – the original downtown that was built over in the 1920s. Or you might want to quench your thirst at The World of Coca-Cola. However, much of the state is rural with farms occupying land once held by rich plantation owners in the pre-Civil War days. Stone Mountain is a sculpted rock salute to those Confederate heroes of the Civil War. And though it's called the Peach State, it is actually the world's largest producer of pecans. Kind of nutty!

Capital: Atlanta
Abbreviation: GA
Population (2010): 9,687,653
Total Area: 58,921 sq. mi. (152,605 sq. km)
State Motto: "Wisdom, Justice and Moderation"
State Bird: Brown Thrasher
State Flower: Cherokee Rose
Sights to See: Savannah – City Squares, The Pirates' House; Atlanta – The Underground, The World of Coca-Cola, Georgia Aquarium, CNN Center; Stone Mountain

KENTUCKY (1792)
Bluegrass State

Kentucky's Cumberland Gap was an entry point for many settlers heading into the frontier. A couple of these settlers were the parents of Abraham Lincoln, who was born in Hodgenville. If you visit the Mountain Life Museum, you can get a taste of what life was like in the early 1800s for Honest Abe. Those settlers established farms over much of Kentucky. But below the surface is the longest known cave system in the world, Mammoth Cave. Kentucky is also home to the famous Kentucky Derby at Churchill Downs. Baseball fans often flock to the classic Louisville Slugger factory in… Louisville. Even the classic American sports car, the Corvette, is manufactured in Bowling Green!

Capital: Frankfort
Abbreviation: KY
Population (2010): 4,339,367
Total Area: 40,411 sq. mi. (104,664 sq. km)
State Motto: "United We Stand, Divided We Fall"
State Bird: Northern Cardinal
State Flower: Goldenrod
Sights to See: Mammoth Cave; Hodgenville – Abraham Lincoln Birthplace; Louisville – Churchill Downs, Louisville Slugger Museum; London – Mountain Life Museum; Land Between The Lakes; Cumberland Gap

TENNESSEE (1796)
Volunteer State

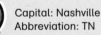

Large numbers of men from Tennessee volunteered to serve in the U.S. Army during the War of 1812. Soon Tennessee was known as the "Volunteer State." Home to President Andrew Jackson, the state was later the site of a number of Civil War battles such as Shiloh, Murfreesboro, and Franklin. Music soon took hold of the state, and both Memphis and Nashville are filled with singers and songwriters. Memphis, on the banks of the Mississippi River, is known as the "Birthplace of the Blues." Elvis Presley made his home there called Graceland. Nashville is world-famous as the center of country music. It's often called Music City, U.S.A. Bristol, in the east, is also known as a music center. You could say Tennessee has a song in its heart!

Capital: Nashville
Abbreviation: TN
Population (2010): 6,346,105
Total Area: 42,145 sq. mi. (109,155 sq. km)
State Motto: "Agriculture and Commerce"
State Bird: Northern Mockingbird
State Flower: Iris
Sights to See: Nashville – Broadway (Honky Tonk Row), Grand Ole Opry, Ryman Auditorium, Country Music Hall of Fame; Memphis – Beale Street, Graceland (Elvis Presley's home); Gatlinburg/Pigeon Forge; Great Smoky Mountains National Park; Chattanooga – Tennessee Aquarium, Chattanooga Choo Choo

ARKANSAS (1836)
The Natural State

Arkansas is a land of lakes, rivers, and mountains. No wonder it's called the Natural State. The Mississippi River makes up most of the western boundary of the state. The Ozark Mountains in the north and Ouachita Mountains in the south are filled with natural beauty. One of the largest springs in America, Mammoth Spring, is also found in the state. Water pours out of the spring at a rate of nine million gallons per hour! One gem of an attraction is the Crater of Diamonds State Park where you can dig for your own diamond! The only flawless diamond in the world, the Strawn-Wagner diamond, was found there. And if you just want to take it easy, try plopping down in the relaxing waters at Hot Springs National Park!

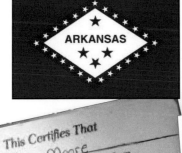

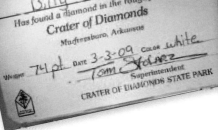

LOUISIANA (1812)
Pelican State / Creole State / Sugar State

Louisiana was the first territory purchased by the young United States of America. France sold the territory, but the French influence has never left the state. The annual Mardi Gras celebration was actually brought to America by the French. Louisiana Creole, as well as Cajun French, are still spoken in the backwater bayous and parishes. They call the area Arcadiana, and it even has its own flag. There's also a French Quarter of New Orleans where a few original French colonial buildings still exist. You can even board an old-style steamboat, like the *Natchez*, and cruise up the Mississippi. Want a feel for the old plantations of the South? You may want to go to White Castle and visit the restored Nottoway Plantation. It's a real Southern Belle!

Capital: Jackson
Abbreviation: MS
Population (2010): 2,967,297
Total Area: 47,692 sq. mi. (123,522 sq. km)
State Motto: "Virtute et Armis (By Valor and Arms)"
State Bird: Northern Mockingbird
State Flower: Southern Magnolia
Sights to See: Natchez – St. Mary's Cathedral,
Longwood Plantation; Vicksburg – Military Park;
U.S.S. *Cairo* ironclad ship; Natchez Trace Parkway;
Jackson – Mississippi Natural History Museum;
Tupelo – Elvis Presley's birthplace; Biloxi

Magnolia State

Mississippi got its nickname from the state tree, the Magnolia. The Mississippi River also serves as the state's western border. It is a land with fertile imaginations. The early settlers created large plantations where sugar, cotton, and tobacco were king. Many people became rich and built large homes or mansions which can be found all across the state. During the Civil War, many battles were fought in Mississippi. The most important battle was fought in Vicksburg for control of the Mississippi River. Today, you can tour the city and even see one of the first armored ships, called an ironclad, the U.S.S. *Cairo*. Music fans may want to visit Elvis Presley's birthplace in Tupelo. Or if you want to get a taste of the Gulf Coast life, you can hop on a shrimping boat tour in Biloxi. Anywhere you go, you'll find warm Southern hospitality and charm!

ALABAMA (1819)

The Heart of Dixie / Cotton State / Yellowhammer State

Alabama has been called the "Heart of Dixie" since the early 1800s. Cotton has always been king here. Its capital, Montgomery, was the original capital of the Confederate States of America. Jefferson Davis was actually inaugurated there as the first (and only) president of the C.S.A. in the state capitol building. Since the Civil War, Alabama slowly forged a new image. They built the rockets that got men to the Moon in Huntsville at the Marshall Space Center. There's even a museum where you can see real rockets, planes, and the space shuttle test vehicle, *Pathfinder*. If you like fast cars, you may want to head to Talladega where NASCAR's finest race. Or just head to Mobile where the U.S.S. *Alabama* is docked year-round.

Capital: Montgomery
Abbreviation: AL
Population (2010): 4,779,736
Total Area: 51,701 sq. mi. (133,905 sq. km)
State Motto: "We Dare Defend Our Rights"
State Bird: Yellowhammer
State Flower: Common Camellia
Sights to See: Huntsville – U.S. Space & Rocket Center/Davidson Center for Space Exploration; Gadsden – Noccalula Falls; Birmingham – Botanical Gardens; Montgomery – Historic State Capitol; Mobile – U.S.S. *Alabama* Battleship; Fort Morgan; Talladega – Talladega Superspeedway

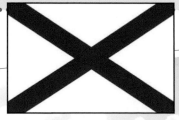

FLORIDA (1845)
Sunshine State

Florida first welcomed visitors way back in 1513. Spanish explorer Juan Ponce de Leon was searching for the legendary Fountain of Youth. Spain established many settlements including St. Augustine in 1565, the oldest city in America. They call Florida the "Sunshine State," but it also has some of the worst storms in the nation. Hurricanes often hit Florida shores, and it has the most lightning strikes of any state. But the visitors keep coming. They flock to Florida's beautiful beaches, theme parks, and natural wonders like the Everglades National ... Kennedy Space Center is found here along with the ...ona International Raceway. ...i and the Florida Keys enjoy ...cal weather like much of ...Caribbean. That means lots ...in and sun. It also means ...n, strawberries, and more. In ...rica is grown in the state and ...ou live, you can always get a

THE CARIBBEAN TERRITORIES
PUERTO RICO (1898)
U.S. VIRGIN ISLANDS
ST. CROIX, ST. THOMAS, ST. JOHN (1917)

Many people are unaware that Puerto Rico is actually part of the United States. It is not a state, but a commonwealth, with a governor. The island was ruled by Spain for over 400 years, but was ceded, or given to the U.S., in 1898 after the Spanish-American War. The Spanish influence is still strong on the island, though. Old Spanish forts are found in several places on the island. Of course, most people today love to visit Puerto Rico's beaches, bays, and rainforests.

Capital: San Juan
Abbreviation: PR
Population (2010 est.): 3,979,000
Official Languages: Spanish; English
Total Area: 3,515 sq. mi. (9,104 sq. km)
Form of Government: Self-governing commonwealth in association with the United States with a Senate and a House of Representatives, similar to most U.S. states with an elected governor.

Capital: Charlotte Amalie
Abbreviation: VI
Population (2010 est.): 109,750
Official Language: English
Total Area: 136 sq. mi. (353 sq. km)
Form of Government: Organized unincorporated territory of the United States with one legislative house (Senate) and an elected governor.
Sights to See: Puerto Rico San Juan – Fort San Felipe del Morro; Vieques Island – Vieques Biobay; El Yunque Tropical Rainforest U.S. Virgin Islands St. Johns – Trunk Bay, Virgin Islands National Park; St. Thomas – Magens Bay, Charlotte Amalie – Blackbeard's Castle; St. Croix – Buck Island Reef National Monument, Frederiksted – Fort Frederik

The U.S. Virgin Islands were actually purchased by the United States from Denmark in 1916 during World War I. The U.S. wanted to keep Germany from building submarine bases there. Of course, the beauty of the Islands makes it hard to think of war today. Cruise ships visit regularly. They bring lots of vacationing tourists from all over the world to sample sunny days in the Caribbean paradise!

THE MIDWEST

The Heartland of America

The Midwest is called the "Heartland" for more than one reason. It's located in the middle of the country. It's also where the heart and soul of the American Dream played out during the 1800s. Much of the area was a vast plain filled with buffalo. Settlers pushed out further and further West. There were clashes with Native American tribes that ended badly. Both sides took losses. Sadly, the Native Americans were forced onto reservations where many live to this day.

Today, the plains and prairies are filled with farms and ranches. The "Heartland" is the center of U.S. agriculture. It's often called the "breadbasket" of America since so much is grown here. Corn is king, followed by wheat and other grains. Large cities are few and far between. Most of the region is dotted with small towns filled with American ingenuity and character. And the people tend to be open, friendly, and hard-working.

The Great Lakes

The Great Lakes have always been a huge industrial center for the United States. Cities like Chicago, Milwaukee, Detroit, and Cleveland sprung up along the shores of the lakes. Waterways and canals were created to link the lakes with rivers and, eventually, the ocean. This meant things made there could be shipped all over the country and the world. Many large companies made the Great Lakes region their home. Companies like International Harvester, Standard Oil, United States Steel, Montgomery Ward, Sears Roebuck, Ford Motor Company, and General Motors are all located here.

The Lakes themselves contain about 21% of the world's fresh water supply (and about 84% of North America's supply). Many of the areas surrounding the lakes were carved by ancient glaciers. That is part of the reason much of the land is so rich with nutrients. That makes the Great Lakes area a fertile farmland as well!

OHIO (1803)
Buckeye State

Capital: Columbus
Abbreviation: OH
Population (2010): 11,536,504
Total Area: 44,825 sq. mi. (116,096 sq. km)
State Motto: "With God, All Things Are Possible"
State Bird: Northern Cardinal
State Flower: Scarlet Carnation
Sights to See: Cleveland – Rock and Roll Hall of Fame; Canton – Pro Football Hall of Fame; Lake Erie; Sandusky – Cedar Point Amusement Park; Berlin – Amish Country; Dayton – U.S. Air Force Museum

So what's a "buckeye"? It's actually the state tree of Ohio. The state is covered with trees and farmland. However, it is also a state where a lot of goods are manufactured. Ohio has lots of natural resources and energy sources such as coal, oil, natural gas, salt, clay, and more. This means they don't have to rely on other states for the materials they need to make things. They also know how to play as hard as they work. In fact, if you like roller coasters, Sandusky is home to Cedar Point Amusement Park – the roller coaster capital of the world! Ohio is also the place to go for some really cool museums. There's the Pro Football Hall of Fame in Canton, the Rock and Roll Hall of Fame in Cleveland, and the U.S. Air Force Museum near the Wright brothers' hometown of Dayton. There are over 360 planes and missiles on display there with a large section devoted to aviation pioneers such as Wilbur and Orville Wright. You could say Ohio has the "Wright" stuff!

INDIANA (1816)
Hoosier State

Some people think a "hoosier" is a basketball player from Indiana. Turns out "hoosier" was once a term the British used to make fun of simple people who lived in the country – like Indiana – back in the 1700s. Today, though, the people of Indiana are proud of their heritage and the name "hoosier." The state is a melting pot of cultures and places. The town of Santa Claus celebrates Christmas year-round.

Capital: Indianapolis
Abbreviation: IN
Population (2010): 6,483,802
Total Area: 36,417 sq. mi. (94,320 sq. km)
State Motto: "Crossroads of America"
State Bird: Northern Cardinal
State Flower: Peony
Sights to See: Indianapolis – Indianapolis Motor Speedway; South Bend – College Football Hall of Fame, Notre Dame University; Lawrenceburg – Perfect North Slopes; Santa Claus – Holiday World; Nappanee – Amish Acres

The town of Nappanee features Amish Acres where you can see how people live a simple lifestyle without electricity. Indiana is also called the "Crossroads of America" since so many people travel through the state. They also race at the Indianapolis Motor Speedway. It's called "The Brickyard" because the track was originally paved with bricks. Whatever the season, Indiana is a state on the move!

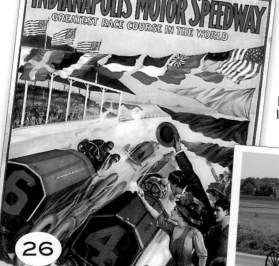

C.G.FISHER Management

MICHIGAN (1837)
Wolverine State / Great Lake State

Michigan is surrounded and divided by four of the five Great Lakes. Lake Superior, Lake Huron, Lake Erie, and Lake Michigan all border the state. Like several of its neighbors, Michigan is known for manufacturing. Detroit is called Motor City since it has been home to many automobile factories dating back to the days of Henry Ford. But Ford did more than build cars. He built the nation's largest indoor/outdoor museum in Dearborn. It's filled with historic buildings like the Edison's lab and the Wright brothers' bicycle shop arranged in a village. Michigan is also filled with natural beauty. Mackinac Island is a sight to behold. But you must travel on foot, bicycle, or horse and buggy. No cars are allowed! And Holland hosts the annual Tulip Festival – one of the largest flower festivals in the country. So in Michigan, you could say things are coming up…tulips!

Capital: Lansing
Abbreviation: MI
Population (2010): 9,883,640
Total Area: 96,713 sq. mi. (250,486 sq. km)
State Motto: "Si Quaeris Peninsulam Amoenam Circumspice (If You Seek a Pleasant Peninsula, Look About You)"
State Bird: American Robin
State Flower: Apple Blossom
Sights to See: Mackinac Island State Park; Holland – Tulip Festival; Dearborn – The Henry Ford Museum and Greenfield Village, Edison Institute; Sault Ste. Marie – Soo Locks; Brooklyn – Michigan International Speedway; Empire – Sleeping Bear Dunes National Lakeshore

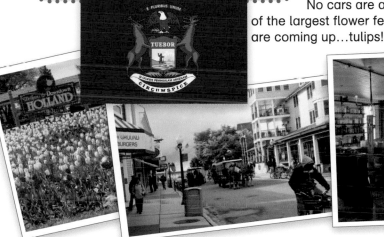

ILLINOIS (1818)
Prairie State / Land of Lincoln

Illinois is definitely the land of Lincoln. The famous president spent much of his life here (though Kentucky gets to claim his birthplace). He's buried near his home in Springfield where you can tour his home and Presidential library. Of course, Chicago is the big attraction in mostly rural Illinois. But the biggest city in Illinois was once the Mormon city of Nauvoo…in 1844. Now Chicago is the big dog and sports a host of attractions. See Sue the T-Rex at the Field Museum. Climb 99 stories to the Willis Tower skydeck for a stunning view of Chicago landscape. Or you can check out all the food and fun at Navy Pier (built in 1916) on Lake Michigan. But no matter what you choose, most people agree that Illinois is more than just a prairie state.

Capital: Springfield
Abbreviation: IL
Population (2010): 12,830,632
Total Area: 57,916 sq. mi. (150,002 sq. km)
State Motto: "State Sovereignty, National Union"
State Bird: Northern Cardinal
State Flower: Violet
Sights to See: Chicago – Field Museum, Willis Tower skydeck, Navy Pier, Oak Park – Frank Lloyd Wright Home & Studio; Nauvoo – Historic Mormon District; Springfield – Abraham Lincoln home, Presidential Library, Lincoln tomb

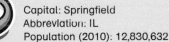

ILLINOIS

WISCONSIN (1848)

Badger State / America's Dairyland

Capital: Madison
Abbreviation: WI
Population (2010): 5,686,986
Total Area: 65,496 sq. mi. (169,634 sq. km)
State Motto: "Forward"
State Bird: American Robin
State Flower: Wood Violet
Sights to See: Wisconsin Dells; Ripon – Little White Schoolhouse a.k.a. Republican Party Birthplace; Spring Green – House On The Rock; Wauwatosa Harley-Davidson Motorcycle Factory; Door County – Sturgeon Bay

Wisconsin celebrates its rich agricultural heritage. That's why it calls itself "America's Dairyland." Wisconsin is quite famous for its dairy products, especially its cheese. It produces more cheese than any other state in America. It's also the second highest milk producer (California is the top producer). No wonder the fans of the Green Bay Packers happily call themselves "Cheese Heads." Wisconsin is also the biggest producer of…water parks! You can cool off any time of the year in Wisconsin Dells. The city is home to over a dozen water parks including one of the world's biggest – Noah's Ark. Some are indoors, some outdoors, but it's definitely a water park wonderland. So in Wisconsin, it's not all about the cheese.

MINNESOTA (1858)

North Star State / Gopher State / Land of 10,000 Lakes / Land of Sky-Blue Waters

Minnesota was the word the Dakota Indians used to describe this land of 10,000 lakes. It means land of sky-blue waters. The early settlements of Minnesota often grew around rivers where they built mills to cut lumber or to grind wheat – two big products for the state. Companies such as General Mills and Pillsbury got their start here. More than half the state lives in the Minneapolis-St. Paul area. The rest of population enjoys the more rural prairies and forests. In fact, most Minnesotans are very active. They enjoy the outdoors in places like Boundary Waters Canoe Area Wilderness. In the winter you might find them ice fishing or hanging out at the Mall of America – a huge mall with a theme park inside! Nothing slows down the people of Minnesota!

Capital: St. Paul
Abbreviation: MN
Population (2010): 5,303,925
Total Area: 86,935 sq. mi. (225,161 sq. km)
State Motto: "L'Étoile du Nord (The North Star)"
State Bird: Common Loon
State Flower: Pink and White Lady's Slipper
Sights to See: Boundary Waters Canoe Area Wilderness; Bloomington – Mall of America; Duluth – Canal Park, Spirit Mountain, Superior National Forest; Mankato – Mount Kato; Judge C. R. Magney State Park – Devil's Kettle Falls

IOWA (1846)
Hawkeye State / Corn State

The Hawkeye State got its nickname from Black Hawk. He was a Sauk Indian whose courage inspired Native Americans and Whites alike. The Sauks were some of the first to farm Iowa. They wouldn't be the last. Many consider Iowa the food capital of the world. It produces more corn than any other state. Iowa also raises a lot of America's hogs, eggs, and soybeans. Food is not all it produces, though. It also harvests the power of the wind using giant wind turbines. Of course, the cities are filled with fun things to see and do. Visit Pella and you can see Dutch architecture and windmills. Burlington has the most crooked street in the world called Snake Alley. Or check out what life was like on the Mississippi way-back-when in Dubuque. Stick around long enough and Iowa just might grow on you!

MISSOURI (1821)
Show-Me State

Missouri was originally part of the Louisiana Purchase in 1803. At that time, St. Louis had already been settled by the French for almost 40 years. Soon the city was called the "Gateway to the West," since explorers and pioneers often began their journeys in St. Louis. Today, the Gateway Arch stands as a very visible monument to the Westward Expansion of America. Missouri was also home to author Mark Twain, and his boyhood home can be found in Hannibal. Twain based much of his writing on his childhood in this town. Of course, Missouri would not be much of a "show-me" state without a "show-me" city. Branson, in the Ozark Mountains, fits that description with a host of shows, restaurants and attractions sure to please any visitor to Missouri.

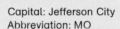

NORTH DAKOTA (1889)
Flickertail State / Sioux State
Peace Garden State

Capital: Bismarck
Abbreviation: ND
Population (2010): 672,591
Total Area: 70,698 sq. mi. (183,107 sq. km)
State Motto: "Liberty and Union, Now and Forever, One and Inseparable"
State Bird: Western Meadowlark
State Flower: Wild Prairie Rose
Sights to See: Buford – Fort Union Trading Post National Historic Site; Medora – Theodore Roosevelt National Park; Jamestown – National Buffalo Museum, Frontier Village; Dunseith – International Peace Garden

North Dakota has always been a place where different cultures encountered each other. Places like Fort Union Trading Post on the Missouri River became a place of peaceful trading between Native American tribes and the white settlers. Farms and ranches now occupy the prairies where great herds of buffalo once roamed. Buffalo can still be found in Theodore Roosevelt National Park where new herds roam the plains. In Jamestown you can visit the National Buffalo Museum. There you can see White Cloud, the sacred white buffalo. The Lakota Indians believe the white buffalo to be a sign of peace, harmony, and balance. The International Peace Garden on the Canadian border is another place where people can come together to celebrate peace. There you can walk back and forth across the border as you enjoy the beautiful scenery and hope for the future shared by two nations!

SOUTH DAKOTA (1889)
Monument State

People have flocked to South Dakota ever since Colonel George A. Custer's men found gold in the Black Hills. Their discovery triggered a gold rush and a costly war with several Native American tribes led by Crazy Horse. The memory of his fighting spirit is carved into the rock at Crazy Horse Memorial. Not far away are the famous stone carvings of U.S. Presidents at Mount Rushmore. Historic Deadwood is the place to go if you want to get a feel for the Wild West. There are also natural monuments in South Dakota. Badlands National Park features amazing rock formations. Custer State Park is a great place to see wildlife. And no trip to South Dakota is complete without a stop at the Corn Palace in Mitchell. No wonder it's called the Monument State.

Capital: Pierre
Abbreviation: SD
Population (2010): 814,180
Total Area: 77,116 sq. mi. (199,730 sq. km)
State Motto: "Under God the People Rule"
State Bird: Ring-Necked Pheasant
State Flower: American Pasqueflower
Sights to See: Keystone – Mount Rushmore; Crazy Horse – Crazy Horse Memorial; Mitchell – Corn Palace; Historic Deadwood; Badlands National Park; Custer – Custer State Park; Wind Cave National Park

NEBRASKA (1867)
Cornhusker State / Beef State

Capital: Lincoln
Abbreviation: NE
Population (2010): 1,826,341
Total Area: 77,349 sq. mi. (200,333 sq. km)
State Motto: "Equality Before the Law"
State Bird: Western Meadowlark
State Flower: Giant Goldenrod
Sights to See: Gering – Scotts Bluff National Monument; Chimney Rock; Beatrice – Homestead National Monument of America; Ogallala – Boot Hill, Mansion on the Hill

Nebraska is one of the most rural states in the country. That's because it's always been a fertile land for farms and cattle. Nebraska actually has a greater heritage as a national highway. The Oregon and Mormon Trails both cross the state. Evidence of their visits can be seen at Scotts Bluff and Chimney Rock – both natural markers of the pioneers' journey. Even the transcontinental railroad ran through Nebraska. Omaha is still the headquarters of the Union Pacific Railroad. Of course, many decided to stay in Nebraska for the free land offered by the Homestead Act of 1862. In Beatrice, you can see an actual homestead site. The products of those homesteads continue to grow and feed America today!

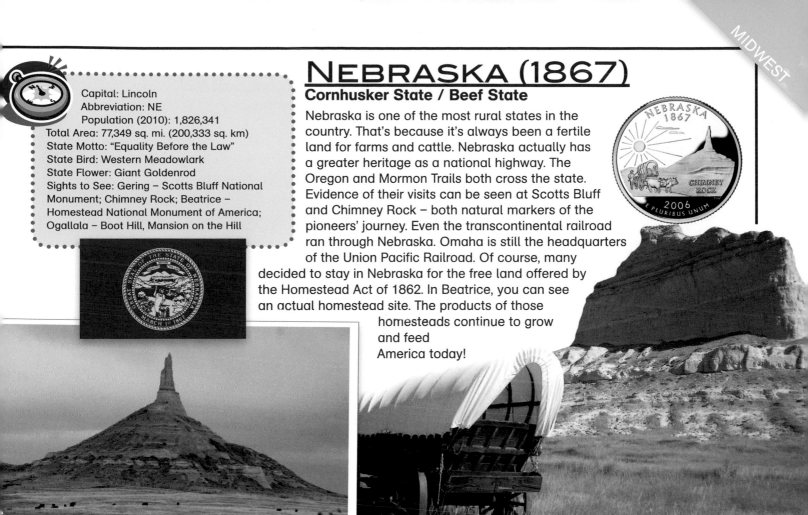

KANSAS (1861)
Sunflower State / Jayhawker State

Kansas has always played a role in the growth of America. Pioneers following the Santa Fe and Oregon Trails regularly traveled through the state. Cattle ranchers from Texas drove their cattle along the famous Chisholm Trail to Abilene and Dodge City to ship them to market. Today, you can stop by these "cowtowns" and see where the west got wild. Or visit Wichita's Old Cowtown Museum for a living history lesson with actors in costume. You can also stop by Topeka for more hands-on history with a full-size steam train at the Kansas History Museum. Today, Kansas is probably known more for agriculture. It grows much of America's wheat and beef. It is also known for wild weather. Kansas is part of an area of the U.S. called Tornado Alley since it has over 50 tornadoes a year. Maybe that's why the name Kansas means "people of the wind!"

Capital: Topeka
Abbreviation: KS
Population (2010): 2,853,118
Total Area: 82,278 sq. mi. (213,099 sq. km)
State Motto: "Ad Astra Per Aspera (To the Stars Through Difficulties)"
State Bird: Western Meadowlark
State Flower: Common Sunflower
Sights to See: Dodge City – Boot Hill Museum; Wichita – Cowtown, Keeper of the Plains; Topeka – Kansas Museum of History; Lawrence – Old West Lawrence; Hutchinson – Kansas Underground Salt Mine/Museum

KANSAS

THE SOUTHWEST

Canyons, Mesas, and Tumbleweeds

The Southwest is a harsh land. It was once host to wayward outlaws and Native Americans on the run. The Apache warrior, Geronimo, held off the American and Mexican armies for over a year once in New Mexico. Billy the Kid and his gang rode through the territory. Even famous gunslingers like Wyatt Earp and Doc Holiday found the O.K. Corral in Tombstone, Arizona.

The land itself was hard on anyone brave enough to enter this dusty place. The early tribes of Native Americans found a way to live and thrive here. The Spanish came here in search of gold and silver. Early American settlers came here seeking a new start in a land too harsh for growing anything.

Then dams and canals were built to bring water to the deserts. Soon crops grew in the hot desert sun. Modern inventions like air conditioning and automobiles brought more and more people to the Southwest. The cities of Phoenix, AZ, and Albuquerque, NM, grew at an amazing rate. And it's still growing today.

A FREE GOVERNMENT SERVICE
GRAND CANYON
NATIONAL PARK
U.S. DEPARTMENT OF THE INTERIOR
NATIONAL PARK SERVICE

32

Cowboys, Sooners, and Indians

Texas and Oklahoma have also been tough lands to tame. Mexico had such a hard time with Comanche Indian raids that they opened the land to outsiders. Soon Americans poured into the territory. The population grew to over 10 times the size it was before. Mexico tried to control the new settlers, but they were a defiant bunch. "Remember the Alamo" became their battle cry. Texas fought back and won its independence from Mexico.

Cowboys and ranchers fought to keep their cattle alive during their epic cattle drives across the state. Then oil was discovered. A new wave of people began entering Texas hoping to make a fortune. A host of oil companies sprang up such as Conoco-Phillips, Exxon-Mobil, and Marathon Oil. The oil boom fueled even more growth. Texas just keeps growing to match the big land it calls home.

Settlers in neighboring Oklahoma had their own challenges. Originally, the land was given to several Native American tribes. Soon, the government decided to encourage settlement and gave the land away in great land races, but keeping the land was tough. The weather was not always kind. The Dust Bowl of the 1930s drove many farmers and ranchers away. Those who survived are a tough, but friendly, breed who welcome visitors today!

ARIZONA (1912)
Grand Canyon State

Capital: Phoenix
Abbreviation: AZ
Population (2010): 6,392,017
Total Area: 113,991 sq. mi. (295,235 sq. km)
State Motto: "Ditat Deus (God Enriches)"
State Bird: Cactus Wren
State Flower: Saguaro Cactus Blossom
Sights to See: Grand Canyon; Lake Havasu City – London Bridge; Phoenix – Heard Museum; Meteor Crater; Tombstone – O.K. Corral; Montezuma Castle National Monument; Navajo Nation – Monument Valley; Wupatki National Monument; Oracle Biosphere 2

Arizona is a state of contrasts. Phoenix, in the center of the state, has more days over 100°F (37.7°C) than any other city. Flagstaff, in the north, has more days with low temperatures below freezing than most cities. There are massive Native American reservations throughout the state. The biggest one – Navajo Nations – takes up an area equal in size to West Virginia. The reservation is filled with areas of unspoiled beauty such as Monument Valley. Many famous Hollywood Westerns were filmed there and in other parts of the state. Real cowboys also lived here. Tombstone was where the famous gunfight at the O.K. Corral happened. Yet natural wonders like Meteor Crater – a huge impact crater – cover the state. Ruins of ancient cliff dwellings can be seen at Montezuma Castle National Monument. You can even walk across the famous London Bridge (moved from England) at Lake Havasu City. Arizona is definitely grand! And it even has a Grand Canyon to prove it!

NEW MEXICO (1912)
Land of Enchantment / Sunshine State

It's rumored that New Mexico's nickname, "Land of Enchantment," originally started with the Santa Fe Railroad, yet people have been "enchanted" by New Mexico for centuries. The Pueblo Indians made their home here in places like Chaco Canyon. The Spanish conquistadors lived in the Palace of Governors in Santa Fe. The famous gunslinger, Billy the Kid, lived here and died at Fort Sumner where they have a museum about his life. Even aliens seem to be attracted to New Mexico. Tales of their visits can be seen at Roswell's UFO Museum. Carlsbad Caverns even offers enchantment a mile below the surface. It seems New Mexico is more than enchanting. For some, it's irresistible.

Capital: Santa Fe
Abbreviation: NM
Population (2010): 2,059,179
Total Area: 121,590 sq. mi. (314,917 sq. km)
State Motto: "Crescit Eundo (It Grows As It Goes)"
State Bird: Roadrunner
State Flower: Yucca Flower
Sights to See: Carlsbad – Carlsbad Caverns National Park; Roswell – International UFO Museum; Nageezi – Chaco Culture National Historic Park; Santa Fe – Palace of the Governors; Fort Sumner – Billy the Kid Museum

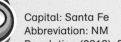

TEXAS (1845)
Lone Star State

Texas is one of a few states that can claim to have once been an independent country. That is why it's called the Lone Star State. The single star reminds it of its struggle for independence from Mexico. The Alamo Mission (a church) in San Antonio was one place where it battled. Eventually, it won and chose to become part of the United States. It is the second biggest state in America. Only Alaska is bigger. Amazingly, cattle ranches and farms cover much of the state. The cities are Texas-big with Houston (4th), San Antonio (7th), and Dallas (9th) in The Top 10 of America's biggest cities. Johnson Space Center in Houston is also the control center for all manned space flights. They even have beaches, like South Padre Island, on the Gulf Coast. But there's nothing quite like a good dance at Guene Hall. It's Texas' oldest, continually-running dance hall, built in 1878. Texas has it all!

Capital: Austin
Abbreviation: TX
Population (2010): 25,145,561
Total Area: 266,833 sq. mi. (691,094 sq. km)
State Motto: "Friendship"
State Bird: Northern Mockingbird
State Flower: Bluebonnet
Sights to See: San Antonio – The Alamo; Paseo del Rio (Riverwalk); Houston – Johnson Space Center; Padre Island National Seashore; New Braunfels – Gruene Hall; Austin – State Capitol Building; Dallas – Cowboy Stadium

OKLAHOMA (1907)
Sooner State

What's a "Sooner"? Well, the government set times when a settler could race for and claim free land in Oklahoma. People who broke the rules and secretly crossed the border early were called… "sooners." And the name stuck! Unfortunately, Oklahoma was also a land of tears. Many Native Americans were forced to move to Oklahoma. They called the trail they traveled the Trail of Tears. Broken Bow has a museum that tells their story. You can also see the grave of the famous Apache warrior, Geronimo, at Fort Sill. Today's "sooners" live in a land filled with twisters (it's part of Tornado Alley). The legacy of the modern cowboy can be found in Oklahoma City at the National Cowboy Hall of Fame and the historic Stockyards City. Through it all, you can say one thing about Oklahoma…its future will always look…OK.

Capital: Oklahoma City
Abbreviation: OK
Population (2010): 3,751,351
Total Area: 69,899 sq. mi. (181,038 sq. km)
State Motto: "Labor Omnia Vincit (Labor Conquers All Things)"
State Bird: Scissor-Tailed Flycatcher
State Flower: American Mistletoe
Sights to See: Oklahoma City – Oklahoma City National Memorial, National Cowboy & Western Heritage Museum, Historic Stockyards; Disney – Pensacola Dam; Fort Sill National Historic Landmark; Broken Bow – Indian Memorial Museum

OKLAHOMA

THE WEST

The Wild West

"Go West" was a cry heard by many of the early pioneers. They ventured into unknown territories hoping to find land and prosperity. What they often found was a lawless land and a fight against the elements.

Of course, the West Coast had been settled by the Spanish in the 1700s, but lands in between were ruled by a gun. The frontier was no place for the weak. Only the strong survived. Gradually, as law and order were established, along with the railroads, the West was opened up!

Today, it is a land of splendor and industry. Silicon Valley in Northern California is a land of technological wonder, yet it's the natural wonders that capture the imagination of most visitors to the West.

New Frontiers

Alaska and its wild territory became part of America back in 1867. Its distance from the rest of the United States kept its wilderness pristine. Then the 1900s brought a gold rush. Years later, oil was discovered. Huge pipelines were built to bring this "black gold" to a hungry market. Yet it's the Alaskan landscapes that are the main attraction today.

Hawaii was an entirely different frontier. Originally, it was country ruled by the grand king of the islands, Kamehameha the Great. Gradually, people came to the islands to work in the sugar cane and pineapple fields. Then the queen was overthrown in 1893, and the country was eventually annexed by the United States. Luckily, the islands still retain their culture and beauty. From the Na Pali Coast to the summit of Mauna Kea, the Hawaiian Islands are a sight to behold!

Guam, the Northern Mariana Islands and American Samoa are also Pacific island gems. Guam and the Northern Mariana Islands were both inhabited by the native Chamorros, and the native language is still spoken today on both islands. American Samoa was originally claimed by the United States but has been allowed to govern itself since 1967. But there is one thing all three territories share — they are all a taste of paradise!

WYOMING (1890)

Equality State

Capital: Cheyenne
Abbreviation: WY
Population (2010): 563,626
Total Area: 97,812 sq. mi. (253,332 sq. km)
State Motto: "Equal Rights"
State Bird: Western Meadowlark
State Flower: Indian Paintbrush
Sights to See: Yellowstone National Park;
Jackson Hole; Grand Tetons National Park;
Hole-in-the-Wall; Devils Tower National
Monument; Cheyenne; Cody – Buffalo Bill
Museum; Laramie – Fort Laramie

Wyoming has always been a land of wonders. Yellowstone National Park was first described by explorer John Colter as a place of "fire and brimstone" in 1807. Most folks thought he was crazy. Turns out he was telling the truth! Today, people from around the world flock to Yellowstone to see wildlife, hot springs, mud pots, and geysers. Others come to see Wyoming's mountains such as the Grand Tetons. Some visit ancient volcanic features like Devils Tower in the northeastern corner of the state. Western outlaws, like Butch Cassidy and the Sundance Kid, came to Wyoming to hide out at Hole-in-the-Wall in the Big Horn Mountains. Even the famous showman, "Buffalo Bill" Cody, liked the state so much he started a town called Cody. That's just the natural attraction that is Wyoming!

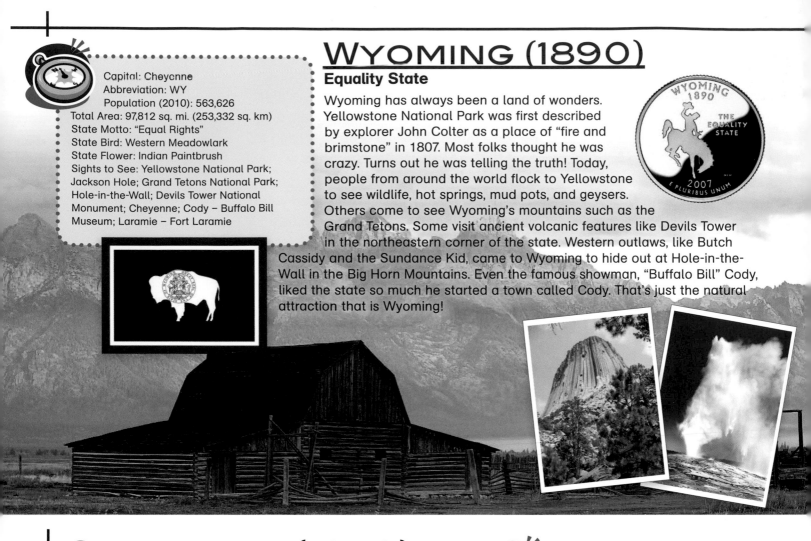

COLORADO (1876)

Centennial State

Colorado is called the Centennial State since it was admitted in 1876 – the 100th anniversary of the United States. Colorado is host to a variety of landscapes. To the south are deserts and Great Sand Dunes National Park. To the east are flat prairies and farm land. To the west are canyon lands like Dinosaur National Monument where fossils are found, or places like Mesa Verde National Park where ancient cliff dwellings can be explored. But the heart of Colorado is its mountains. Over half the state is covered with rocky peaks. More than 800 mountains are over 10,000 feet high. And you don't have to be a mountain climber to enjoy them. Pike's Peak (elevation 14,115 ft / 4,302 m) actually has a road to the top! And the view from the summit inspired Katherine Lee Bates to write the words to "America the Beautiful."

Capital: Denver
Abbreviation: CO
Population (2010): 5,029,196
Total Area: 104,095 sq. mi. (269,605 sq. km)
State Motto: "Nil Sine Numine (Nothing Without
Providence)"
State Bird: Lark Bunting
State Flower: White and Lavender Columbine
Sights to See: Denver – U.S. Mint;
Golden – Colorado Railroad Museum; Dinosaur
– Dinosaur National Monument; Pike's Peak;
Cortez – Mesa Verde National Park; Colorado
Springs – U.S. Air Force Academy; Estes Park
– Rocky Mountain National Park; Great Sand
Dunes National Park and Preserve; Royal Gorge

UTAH (1896)
Beehive State

The name Utah comes from the Ute Indians who lived in the state. The name means "people of the mountains." Anyone who's been to Utah can tell you about the mountains and the "Greatest Snow on Earth" found at the many ski resorts. Utah was settled largely by Mormon pioneers led by Brigham Young in the 1800s. Through their efforts, the desert valleys were turned into productive farm land. They also built a solid granite temple which can be seen in Salt Lake City today. The city also hosted the 2002 Winter Olympics. It was a natural fit with a state that is known for outdoor recreation. National Parks like Zion, Bryce Canyon, and Arches draw thousands of visitors each year. Some even visit Promontory Point where the transcontinental railroad was completed. No wonder they call Utah the "Crossroads of the West."

NEVADA (1864)
Silver State / Sagebrush State
Battle Born State

The "Silver State" got its name long before casinos dotted the desert floor. The discovery of silver at the Comstock Lode in 1859 attracted thousands of people. Just before the discovery, Mormons had built a fort in what would become Las Vegas. Nevada was soon a state, and things were never the same. Mining continued to play a large part in the state's growth, but the largest growth came when the government came to town. Boulder, or Hoover Dam, was built in 1935. It harnessed the power of the Colorado River, providing power to the Las Vegas area and beyond. It also created the biggest man-made lake in America – Lake Mead. Other government projects and military bases came to the state and brought more people with them. Soon, gambling and casinos were added to the mix. Before long, Nevada became the bright and shiny tourist destination it is today!

WASHINGTON (1889)

Evergreen State / Chinook State

Capitul: Olympia
Abbreviation: WA
Population (2010): 6,724,540
Total Area: 68,095 sq. mi. (176,365 sq. km)
State Motto: "Alki (By and By)"
State Bird: Willow Goldfinch
State Flower: Coast Rhododendron
Sights to See: Seattle – Space Needle, Pioneer Square; Olympic National Park; Mount Rainier National Park; Mount St. Helen's National Volcanic Monument

Washington is the only state named after a U.S. President. It is definitely the "Evergreen State." Much of the state is made up of temperate rain forests and old growth trees. Olympic National Park is one place you can see such evergreens. You can also see mountains and ancient glaciers in many places including Mount Rainier National Park. Natural adventure can be found in places like Mount St. Helen's National Volcanic Monument. There you can see a volcano that literally blew its top in 1980. However, the coast is where much of Washington's business happens. Logging, fishing, and high-tech software companies all call the Puget Sound area home. Seattle is the biggest of the cities. Over half the state's population lives, works, and plays there. They go to places like the Space Needle (605 ft./184 m) or Pioneer Square where you can see a real totem pole. Just remember to bring an umbrella, the Washington coast is one of the rainiest places in America!

OREGON (1859)

Beaver State

Explorers Lewis and Clark navigated the Columbia River in their famous journey to map the Louisiana Purchase. They weren't the first adventurers to reach Oregon, and they weren't the last either. Astoria began as Fort Astoria. It was named after John Jacob Astor of New York who funded the new settlement where they traded in furs. Many of the furs came from beavers, which is where the state gets its nickname. Today's Oregon travelers come for a variety of reasons. Some want to see nature's handiwork at Crater Lake National Park, Mount Bachelor, or Multnomah Falls in Troutdale. You can even snow ski year-round at Mount Hood due to its many glaciers. On the coast there are wonders such as the Heceta Head Light or Sea Lion Cave, both near Florence. Sea Lion Cave is one of the great sea cave grottos of the world with a 125 ft. (38 m) high vaulted stone ceiling and...sea lions!

Capital: Salem
Abbreviation: OR
Population (2010): 3,831,074
Total Area: 97,048 sq. mi. (251,353 sq. km)
State Motto: "Alis Volat Propoiis (She Flies with Her Own Wings)"
State Bird: Western Meadowlark
State Flower: Oregon Grape
Sights to See: Mount Hood; Crater Lake National Park; Astoria – Fort Astoria, Columbia River Maritime Museum; Mt. Bachelor; Portland – International Rose Test Garden; Florence – Heceta Head Light, Sea Lion Cave; Troutdale – Multnomah Falls

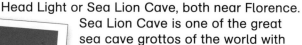

IDAHO (1890)
Gem State

Every known gemstone has been found in the state of Idaho. That's how it got the name, "Gem State." In fact, the rare star garnets can only be found in two places on the planet – India and Idaho. Of course, they're not the only Idaho gems. Astronauts used to train on the lava landscapes at Craters of the Moon National Monument since it is very similar to…the moon. Today, visitors can explore the other-worldly landscape filled with cinder cones and lava tube caves. Sun Valley in central Idaho is one of the state's snow skiing and recreation gems. Shoshone Falls in Twin Falls is another overlooked gem. At a height of 212 ft. (65 m), it is actually higher than the more famous Niagara Falls. And few people know that Lewistown, Idaho, is a true seaport. The Snake and Columbia Rivers actually connect it to the Pacific Ocean. Of course, Idaho's most famous gem is the potato that it ships to destinations all over the country!

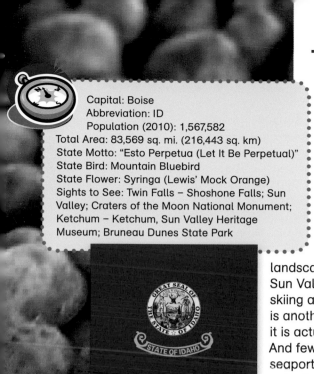

MONTANA (1889)
Big Sky Country / Treasure State

Montana has two nicknames for the two distinct sections of the state. The west gives Montana its name as a "Treasure State." One of the largest U.S. gold deposits was found at Adler Gulch (now called Virginia City). Glacier National Park with its beautiful lakes and mountains is a national treasure. Lewis and Clark Caverns is another treasure that, strangely enough, was never visited by the famous explorers. They did visit Pompey's Pillar, though. Like many pioneers and explorers, William Clark carved his name into the sandstone pillar which can still be seen to this day. Not far away is the site of Custer's Last Stand at Little Bighorn Battlefield National Monument. "Big Sky Country" refers more to eastern Montana with its prairies and flat plains. Of course, you could call the whole state dinosaur country for the fossils found throughout!

MONTANA

SEE AMERICA
WELCOME TO MONTANA
UNITED STATES TRAVEL BUREAU

CALIFORNIA (1850)
Golden State

Capital: Sacramento
Abbreviation: CA
Population (2010): 37,253,956
Total Area: 158,608 sq. mi. (410,793 sq. km)
State Motto: "Eureka (I Have Found It)"
State Bird: California Valley Quail
State Flower: California Poppy
Sights to See: Yosemite National Park; Sequoia National Park; Kings Canyon National Park San Franscisco – Golden Gate Bridge, Fisherman's Wharf, Alcatraz Island; Old Spanish Missions, El Camino Real; Big Sur; Disneyland; Hollywood – Grauman's Chinese Theater, Walk of Fame; Santa Monica Pier; San Diego Zoo

The discovery of gold at Sutter's Mill in 1848 is just one of the reasons California is called the "Golden State." The golden sands of the 840-mile (1352 km) shoreline with its beautiful beaches, like Malibu or Big Sur, call to many. The Central Valley produces agricultural gold with its variety of fruits and vegetables. California also produces box-office gold from its dream factories in Hollywood. Of course, the gold standard for outdoor beauty is found in places like Yosemite and Sequoia/Kings Canyon National Parks or the Sierra Nevada Mountains with Lake Tahoe. Tourists can't help but be drawn to classic attractions like Disneyland, the historic chain of Spanish Missions, the Santa Monica Pier, or the Golden Gate Bridge in San Francisco. California is truly gold from its rich history to its land and sunny weather. Even if there is an occasional earthquake, the rush for California gold continues today!

CALIFORNIA REPUBLIC

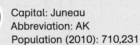

ALASKA (1959)
The Last Frontier

Capital: Juneau
Abbreviation: AK
Population (2010): 710,231
Total Area: 590,693 sq. mi. (1,529,888 sq. km)
State Motto: "North to the Future"
State Bird: Willow Ptarmigan
State Flower: Alpine Forget-Me-Not
Sights to See: Denali National Park/Mount McKinley (Denali); Iditarod Trail Sled Dog Race; Kenai Fjords National Park; Glacier Bay; Kodiak Island; Chugach State Park; Fairbanks – El Dorado Gold Mine; Anchorage – Alaska Native Heritage Center

Alaska is truly the "Last Frontier" in America. One look at Denali National Park and you'll know you're in a whole new world. The state is home to a host of wildlife including caribou, moose, bears (grizzly, black and polar), wolves, eagles (bald, golden), seals, and sea otters. Alaska is the biggest state in the Union. Many visitors arrive on cruise ships to see icebergs calve (break away) into Glacier Bay or the fjords of Kenai Fjords National Park. Or you could use the original native Aleut method of travel – dog sleds! Of course, you may just want to watch annual Iditarod Trail Sled Dog Race without enduring the harsh winter weather. And if you want to get a feel for the Klondike Gold Rush of 1897, you can visit El Dorado Gold Mine in Fairbanks. In order to see Alaska through native eyes, you need to stop at the Alaska Native Heritage Center in Anchorage. They may even teach you to say "Aang-Aleut" (Aleut for "Hello")!

HAWAII (1959)

Aloha State

Capital: Honolulu
Abbreviation: HI
Population (2010): 1,360,301
Total Area: 6,468 sq. mi. (16,752 sq. km)
State Motto: "Ua Mau Ke Ea O Ka Aina I Ka Pono (The Life of the Land Is Perpetuated in Righteousness)"
State Bird: Nene (Hawaiian Goose)
State Flower: Yellow Hibiscus
Sights to See: Big Island (Hawai'i) – Hawaii Volanoes National Park (Mt. Kilauea), Pu`uhonua o Honaunau National Historical Park; O'ahu – Polynesian Cultural Center, Pearl Harbor (U.S.S. *Arizona* Memorial), Hanauma Bay Nature Preserve; Kaua'i – Na Pali Coast, Waimea Canyon, Kalalau Lookout; Maui – Haleakala National Park

Hawai'i first said, "Aloha," to visitors in 1778 when British explorer James Cook landed on the Big Island (Hawai'i). "Aloha" means both "hello" as well as "goodbye" in the Hawaiian language. The state is also made up of several islands – Hawai'i (the Big Island), Maui, Kaho'olawe, Lana'i, Moloka'i, O'ahu, Kaua'i, and Ni'ihau. Hawai'i is known for its amazing natural wonders. The Big Island is host to active volcanoes and lava flows at Hawaii Volcanoes National Park. Or go to Kaua'i and see its Na Pali Coast or Waimea Canyon – the Grand Canyon of the Pacific. Look no further than the Polynesian Cultural Center for a fun luau (Hawaiian feast) where you might even learn to hula (a native dance). Of course, the beaches are fabulous. Some even have black sand from volcanic rock! And don't forget to snorkel on the coral reefs of Hanauma Bay Nature Preserve. Soon you'll see why this state has been called "paradise"!

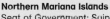

THE PACIFIC TERRITORIES

Guam (acquired 1898), Northern Mariana Islands (admitted 1978, U.S. Commonwealth)
American Samoa (acquired 1899, self-governing since 1967)

Guam
Capital: Hagåtña (formerly Agaña)
Population (2010 est.): 187,000
Official Languages: Chamorro; English
Total Area: 217 sq. mi. (561 sq. km)
Head of State: President of the United States
Form of Government: Self-governing, organized, unincorporated territory of the United States with one legislative body (Legislature) and a governor.
Monetary Unit: U.S. Dollar

Northern Mariana Islands
Seat of Government: Saipan
Population (2010 est.): 48,300
Official Languages: Chamorro; Carolinian; English
Total Area: 176.5 sq. mi. (457.1 sq. km)
Head of State: President of the United States
Form of Government: Self-governing commonwealth in association with the United States, having two legislative houses (Senate; House of Representatives)
Monetary Unit: U.S. Dollar

American Samoa
Capital: Fagatogo (legislative and judicial) and Utulei (executive)
Population (2010 est.): 65,900
Official Languages: English; Samoan
Total Area: 77 sq. mi. (200 sq. km)
Form of Government: Unincorporated and unorganized territory of the United States with two legislative houses (Senate and House of Representatives) and a governor
Monetary Unit: U.S. Dollar

Guam was once part of Spain, and its influence can be seen in the Dulce Nombre De Maria Cathedral Basilica. The island hosts major U.S. military bases today. It's also part of "Typhoon Alley." Many homes are made with reinforced concrete to withstand the hurricane-strength storms. And if you want a taste of the native culture, be sure to visit the Chamorro Village Market on Wednesdays for food and entertainment that can only be found in Guam!

The Northern Mariana Islands are made up of 15 islands just north of Guam. Several of the islands have active volcanoes on them. The beaches are beautiful as well as the coral reefs, especially on Mañagaha Island where the famous Caroline Islands Chief Aghurubw is buried!

American Samoa shares many of the same features and culture as its cousin, the country of Samoa (also called Western Samoa). In fact, the traditional birthplace of Samoa is found within the territory at the Manu'a Islands. They are part of the National Park of American Samoa. It is the only national park south of the equator!

GLOSSARY

a.k.a – An abbreviation for "also known as."

Agriculture – The business of farming or raising animals for food.

Amish – Strict Mennonite groups, mostly in Pennsylvania, Ohio, Indiana, and Canada, that originally followed Jakob Ammann, a 17th century Swiss Mennonite bishop. In addition to living simple and wearing plain clothes, they do not use modern conveniences like electricity and gas-powered machines.

Bayou – A swampy or slow-moving body of water and the land surrounding it. Bayous are often found in the Deep South in states like Louisiana.

Border – A boundary of a state or country.

Caribbean – Anything to do with the Caribbean Sea and its islands.

City Council – An elected, law-making group of men and women who help run a city or town.

Commonwealth – A large area of land with borders within a country that is like a state.

Conquistadors – Spanish conquerors of Mexico and other parts of North and South America.

County – An area of land smaller than a state, that includes several cities.

Culture – Ideas, activities, and traditions of a group of people, often from another country.

Deep South – The most southern of the Southeastern U.S., especially Alabama, Georgia, Mississippi, South Carolina or Louisiana.

District – An area similar to a state but smaller, such as the District of Columbia.

Dixie – A nickname for the southeastern states adopted from the Mason-Dixon line that created the state boundaries between the free state of Pennsylvania and the slave state of Missouri.

Elevation – How high or low a land mass is.

Federal Government – The national government of a country.

Fertile – Something (land, imagination) that is able to produce or make more of something than others (for example – fertile soil produces more crops).

Fjords (pronounced "fee-yords") – A long, narrow arm of the sea with steep cliffs or mountains on either side.

Governor – The leader of a state or territory.

Great Lakes – Five large lakes (Lake Superior, Lake Michigan, Lake Huron, Lake Erie and Lake Ontario)

House of Representatives – An elected, law-making group of men and women that is based on the number of people living in each area. This allows states with more people to have the most votes on new laws.

Industry – Making or manufacturing things like cars, computers, steel, or glass, often in a factory.

Ingenuity – The ability to come up with smart ways of doing things.

Key – A small, flat island.

Keystone – The stone or brick at the top center of an arch that holds the arch together.

Landscape – An area of countryside, or land, including all plants and natural features like streams, rivers, hills or mountains, etc.

Louisiana Purchase – Land bought from France in 1803 that doubled the size of the United States. Louisiana and all, or part, of over 14 other states were created from the land.

Mayor – The elected leader of a city.

Melting Pot – A term used to describe many people from different countries, races, and religious beliefs working together to form a shared community or country.

Mennonite – A member of a Protestant faith named after Menno Simons, a 16th century Frisian religious leader. They are noted for their plain clothes and simple living and oppose war or bearing arms.

Mid-Atlantic – An area around the Central Atlantic Coast including Virginia, West Virginia, Delaware, Maryland, New Jersey, Pennsylvania, and New York.

Midwest – An area of the North Central U.S. that is made up of a dozen states from Ohio in the east to the Dakotas in the west. The area also includes many states surrounding the Great Lakes.

Missouri Compromise – A law passed in 1820 that allowed Missouri to be admitted as a slave state and Maine to be admitted as a free state with no slavery allowed further north in the territories such as Nebraska or Kansas.

Mormon – The nickname for a member of the Church of Jesus Christ of Latter-day Saints. The name comes from the Book of Mormon, a book of scripture they use in addition to the Holy Bible.

Nationality – Belonging to a particular country. For example, someone of German nationality would be from Germany.

Natural Resources – Natural materials such as land, forests, water, or minerals (like gold or iron) used to make different things.

New England – The northeast area of the U.S. which includes the states of Vermont, Connecticut, New Hampshire, Rhode Island, Massachusetts, and Maine.

Outer Banks – A 200-mile string of barrier islands off the coast of North Carolina where the Wright Brothers made their first powered flight.

Parish – Another name for a county, usually in the state of Louisiana. Originally, it came from the French and Spanish Catholic Church parishes in the state.

Pilgrims – Protestant settlers that came across the Atlantic Ocean seeking religious freedom in a new land, like America.

Plains – An area of land that is mostly flat. The areas east of the Rocky Mountains in the Central U.S. are called the Great Plains.

Plantation – A very large farm with lots of workers, often in the southern states. Most of the workers were slaves until they were freed during the Civil War.

Prairie – A grassy, mostly flat area of land that has few trees found in the Central United States.

Prosperous – To be successful.

Protestant – A member of any Christian faith that "protested" the changes in the original Catholic, Anglican, or Eastern Orthodox Churches.

Puget Sound – An arm of the Pacific Ocean in northwest Washington State.

Seaport – A town or city on an ocean or river connected to the ocean where goods are loaded or unloaded on ships to be transported to other places.

Senate – An elected, law-making group of men and women where each area has the same number of representatives. This allows smaller states to have an equal vote to the large states on new laws.

Sound – An arm of the ocean that is wider than a fjord and bigger than a bay.

State – A large area of land within a country with borders, like the state of Tennessee in the United States of America.

Tar – A thick, black, sticky substance made of tree sap that drips out of wood when it is heated to a high temperature and turned into wood coal.

U.S. Territory – An area, like a state, that is also part of the United States.

Union – Another name for all the states that have joined together to form the United States of America.

Waterway – A river or canal, sometimes with small moveable dams (called locks) that allow large ships to travel from areas like the Great Lakes to the ocean.

INDEX